Kipfer

BIG
BIG BOATS

by Catherine Ipcizade

Consulting Editor: Gail Saunders-Smith, PhD

CAPSTONE PRESS
a capstone imprint

Pebble Plus is published by Capstone Press,
151 Good Counsel Drive, P.O. Box 669, Mankato, Minnesota 56002.
www.capstonepress.com

092009
005618CGS10

 Books published by Capstone Press are manufactured with paper
containing at least 10 percent post-consumer waste.

Library of Congress Cataloging-in-Publication Data
Ipcizade, Catherine.
    Big boats / by Catherine Ipcizade.
    p. cm. — (Pebble Plus. Big)
    Includes bibliographical references and index.
    Summary: "Simple text and photographs describe big boats" — Provided by publisher.
    ISBN 978-1-4296-3993-4 (library binding)
    1. Boats and boating — Juvenile literature. 2. Ships — Juvenile literature. I. Title. II. Series.
VM150.I63 2010
623.82 — dc22   2009026034

Editorial credits
Erika L. Shores, editor; Ted Williams, designer; Wanda Winch, media researcher; Eric Manske, production specialist

Photo credits
Art Life Images/Walter Bibikow, cover
Courtesy of Jan Oosterboer, shipspotting.com, 1
Courtesy of Pascal Bredel, shipspotting.com, 21
fotolia/Marek Cech, 5
Getty Images Inc./AFP/JiJi Press, 15
iStockphoto/Giovanni Rinaldi, 9
Shutterstock/Artem Samokhvalov, 19; gaga, cover (background); Jim Lopes, 17; Philipe Ancheta, 7
U.S. Navy photo by General Dynamics Electric Boat, 11
U.S. Navy photo/Photographer's Mate 3rd Class David K. Simmons, 13

Capstone Press thanks Naval historian Randy Papadopoulos, PhD, for his assistance in reviewing this book.

Note to Parents and Teachers

The Big set supports national science standards related to science and technology. This book
describes and illustrates big boats. The images support early readers in understanding the
text. The repetition of words and phrases helps early readers learn new words. This book
also introduces early readers to subject-specific vocabulary words, which are defined in the
Glossary section. Early readers may need assistance to read some words and to use the Table of
Contents, Glossary, Read More, Internet Sites, and Index sections of the book.

Table of Contents

Big

From sailboats to submarines,

all kinds of big boats

sail on the sea.

Hydroplanes are
big speedboats.
They almost fly
as they race over water.

Size:
up to 30 feet
(9 meters) long

Sailboats glide

over deep water.

Big sails catch the wind.

Size:

up to 247 feet

(75 meters) long

Bigger

Submarines dive underwater. Big propellers move them through the ocean.

Size:

up to 560 feet (171 meters) long

Destroyers hold big missiles.
The long ships move fast
to attack enemies.

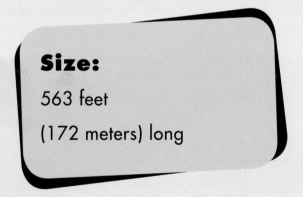

Size:

563 feet
(172 meters) long

Biggest

Fighter jets take off

from an aircraft carrier's deck.

The big deck is longer than

three football fields.

Size:

1,090 feet

(332 meters) long

Cruise ships are

a vacation at sea.

The biggest cruise ships

have up to 1,800 guest rooms.

Size:

up to 1,112 feet
(339 meters) long

Tanker ships carry liquids.
Big oil tankers hold
more than 3 million barrels
of oil.

Size:
up to 1,247 feet
(380 meters) long

Container ships are
the biggest ships at sea.
The ships bring cars, TVs,
and food to people
around the world.

Size:
up to 1,300 feet
(396 meters) long

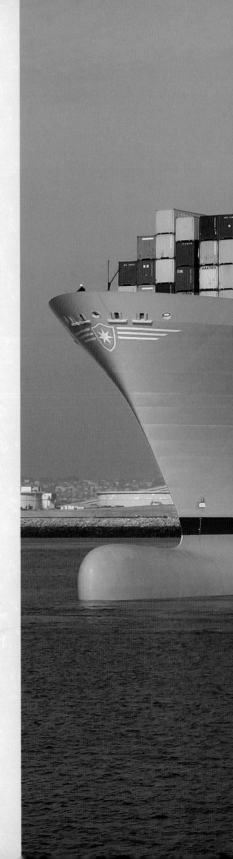

Glossary

barrel — a large container that has curved sides and a flat top and bottom

container — a type of box that can be loaded onto a ship; containers can hold many kinds of goods.

deck — the long, flat area on top of a ship; planes can take off and land on the deck of an aircraft carrier.

missile — a weapon that is fired at a target to blow it up

propeller — a set of spinning blades that pushes submarines and other kinds of boats through water

sail — a large sheet of strong cloth on a boat; a sail catches the wind; the wind pushes the boat forward.

vacation — a trip away from home

Read More

Lindeen, Mary. *Ships*. Mighty Machines. Minneapolis: Bellwether Media, 2007.

Pipe, Jim. *Giant Machines*. Read and Play. Mankato, Minn.: Stargazer Books, 2009.

Tatge, Cathy. *Boats*. My First Look at Vehicles. Mankato, Minn.: Creative Education, 2008.

Internet Sites

FactHound offers a safe, fun way to find Internet sites related to this book. All of the sites on FactHound have been researched by our staff.

Here's all you do:

Visit *www.facthound.com*

FactHound will fetch the best sites for you!

Index

Word Count: 127
Grade: 1
Early-Intervention Level: 14